BUGLE BOY

BUGLE BOY

Len Chester

ISIS
LARGE PRINT
Oxford

First published in Great Britain 2007
by
Long Barn Books

Published in Large Print 2008 by ISIS Publishing Ltd.,
7 Centremead, Osney Mead, Oxford OX2 0ES
by arrangement with
Long Barn Books

British Library Cataloguing in Publication Data
Chester, Len
    Bugle boy. – Large print ed.
    (Isis reminiscence series)
    1. Chester, Len
    2. Great Britain. Royal Marines – History
    3. World War, 1939–1945 – Personal narratives, British
    4. World War, 1939–1945 – Naval operations, British
    5. World War, 1939–1945 – Campaigns – Arctic regions
    6. Child soldiers – Great Britain
    7. Large type books
    I. Title
    940.5'45921'092

        ISBN 978–0–7531–9486–7 (hb)
        ISBN 978–0–7531–9487–4 (pb)

Printed and bound in Great Britain by
T. J. International Ltd., Padstow, Cornwall

To my beloved wife Vera

Foreword by H.R.H. The Duke of Edinburgh
Captain General, The Royal Marines

The individual stories of men who served through wars may not constitute 'history', but these accounts are the stuff of history and they are very valuable material for later historians.

'Bugle Boy' is an eloquent description of the experiences of a boy of just over 14 years after he joined the Royal Marines at the outset of the Second World War. Many others will have had similar experiences, but very few will have put them down on paper as a record for later generations.

Future historians may concentrate on the broader issues of the war, but it is reminiscences like these, which will give them the opportunity to include the human dimension.

Philip

Contents

Preface

I never set out to write a book about World War Two; that has been done so many times by many others. What I have compiled is a series of cameos, stories which over fifty years of married life my beloved wife, Vera, heard so many times and insisted that I record, even if it was only for my children and grandchildren. When Vera died in 1997, the cudgel was taken up by our daughter, Lynne, who nagged and nagged until eventually I sat down to write just to get some peace and quiet. Having done so I am pleased, because how many times have I been told "You must have told some porkies to join up at fourteen years of age" or looked upon with disbelief at the idea that I went to active war at fourteen years and eight months.

Well, we Royal Marine Boy Buglers did. A fact that very few people will know is that Royal Marine Boy Bugler Peter Avant, who died aged fifteen when HMS *Fiji* was sunk during the battle for Crete, was the youngest member of the Armed Forces to be killed on active service during the war. If things had turned out differently on 16 March 1940 I would have held that record as I was still only fourteen, two weeks off my fifteenth birthday.

In this book are just a few events noted by a young boy who became a man long before his time and who lost his youth in the service of his country. We boys had to grow up very quickly or we would not have survived. We may have started lightheartedly, but the seriousness of our situation soon became very apparent. So think of all those boys who died, and there were many of them, and remember them; and if you find interest in what I have written, thank my wife and our daughter, without whose persistence I would never have put pen to paper.

Tavistock, 5 April 2007

The King's Shilling

There are certain days which stay in the memory for ever. For me, the most memorable was the day I left the family bosom to join the Royal Marines. It was 3 May 1939; I was exactly fourteen years and twenty-eight days old and I was about to go from one extreme to the other before that day was over. In true melodrama, I suppose there would have been tears and much wailing from both Mother and Father and, of course, me. But there wasn't; I could have been going off to the Boys' Brigade summer camp for all the sympathy shown. I have often wondered if they felt any sadness at my going — after all there was a war in the offing even if Mr Chamberlain had a piece of paper to prove there wasn't, and I was taking a very small step for mankind, but a giant leap for a small boy (sorry). My mother was a typical London mum and my father was a policeman and a World War One veteran — both, I suspect, bursting with pride to see another son going off to fight the Hun. Maybe it was one less mouth to feed and a way of foisting all the teenage problems of the future on to someone else. I shall never know now.

I too should have felt some sadness, but I didn't —
not that I had an unhappy childhood or I was beaten,
quite the opposite, but from the day I went to see my
brother's King's Squad parade at Chatham (he joined
the Royal Marines in 1937), I knew that all I ever
wanted to be was one of those drummers/buglers. I
applied when I was thirteen and was accepted readily
and told to report to Great Scotland Yard in Whitehall
Place. The Recruiting Sergeant who received me could
have been a Thomas Hardy character, 7'8" tall (or so it
seemed to me) and wide as a tree trunk, wearing a large
rosette in his cap, all smiles and back-slapping and full
of congratulations for the brave decision I had made
("laddie"). I had a very cursory but humiliating
medical and then was taken before an Officer to swear
my allegiance to King and Country and receive the
King's shilling.

Did you know that it was for this that glass-bottomed
tankards were made? In olden days the Recruiting
Sergeant would place a shilling in the pint of beer he so
generously bought for you, and then when you emptied
it you picked out the coin. You were now a soldier or a
sailor, whether you liked it or not; but if the tankard
had a glass bottom you could see the shilling before
touching it. Many potential sailors were not quite so
fortunate; they were battered unconscious and when
they woke up they were probably rounding the Nab
Tower out in the Solent.

I made my oath and received my shilling, but the
Recruiting Sergeant said that my lunch had cost 1s 6d
and that I therefore owed him 6d. Somewhere along

4

the line all the smiles and back-slapping had disappeared and, before I knew what was happening, I was on my way to Eastney Barracks in Portsmouth.

The first pangs of homesickness were beginning to be felt.

Barracks

I have no recollection of arriving at Eastney Barracks. All I can remember is that I left London on an electric train from Waterloo to Portsmouth with six men destined to be Marines, but our actual arrival at the barracks is a blank — maybe the memory does that, putting into the recycle-bin all those things it doesn't want.

I said that I was going to go from one extreme to the other before the day was out and that was certainly true. Remember, I was very young, 4′ 8″ tall and straight from Rowan Road Secondary School, Mitcham, Surrey. I was not a brilliant scholar and had not attained a standard that would have gained me entrance to a grammar school. It must have been very traumatic suddenly to be thrust into this world of men whilst I was still a child in all respects — there were even things about me that had not yet started to grow.

My awakening to reality came when I found myself sat down to tea in a massive high room on a bench at a long wooden table; the other occupants of this Fagin's Kitchen had not yet returned from scavenging or whatever they were up to, so I was on my own and was given a bowl of tea. Now in those days we didn't have central dining rooms, we ate in our barrack rooms where we lived and slept, and we didn't have cups, we drank from bowls, rather Grecian in style but requiring a certain amount of skill to drink from one-handed. You soon learnt that trick as the other hand was on your plate else some other poor urchin would readily have the contents. It was a rough world.

Having drunk the tea somehow and eaten a slice of bread and strawberry jam (why was it always strawberry jam?) followed by a piece of fruit cake, I was taken to an identical room which had about thirty beds in it and shown to an apparently vacant one occupying a space ten feet by eight feet that was to be my little world from now on. Within this are I would eat, sleep and stow all my belongings, which were none at that time.

The bed was a cast-iron framework in two halves, one of which slid under the other and had to be pulled out when laying down the mattress, which was a palliasse, filled with straw. Already I had begun to miss my feather-filled bed; here it was hard, with two white blankets, one brown blanket and two white sheets. My mother, I now realized, had been very remiss in not showing me how to make up a bed. It must have been about 4.30 when all the other occupants of room B2 returned from bugle and drum practice and from then on bedlam reigned, partly, I am sure, to impress the new boy. They all began to do strange things, say strange words, act in strange ways; I was completely out of my depth and could only sit on the bed frame with my mouth wide open and tears pricking my eyelids.

At 7p.m. we were allowed to make our beds, so I watched and copied what the other boys did — I soon became very clever at doing that, a skill that has lasted all my life and made up for not being a brilliant scholar. At 10p.m. we all got into our beds, the lights went out at 10.15 and soon all that could be heard were snores, talkers in their sleep, moans and the breaking of wind. If you listened carefully you would have heard me crying. The pangs of homesickness were really hurting now.

Families

There has always been an element of "families" in the Armed Services; sons followed in their fathers' footsteps, brothers influenced brothers and could at one time ask to serve together until on occasion there were whole families in one branch of the Services. It was more noticeable in the time of World War One, when recruiting drives were done on the spot in towns and villages before the days of radio or television; consequently, whole villages or townships were enrolled in the local regiment. Sometimes this would almost strip a community of its menfolk, and they became known as "Pals" — the best known were the "Accrington Pals". It is easy to see the flaw in this system as in some major battles like the Somme, Passchendaele and Mons 40,000 men could be killed in one day, whole regiments were decimated, a battalion would disappear — in fact all the men of one village would be lost. The "Accrington Pals" were virtually wiped out in one engagement.

The Royal Marines, and also the Royal Navy, had the same problem in World War One and if you visit the Medals Room in the Royal Marines Museum, at

Eastney, Portsmouth, you can see how many families are represented, grandfathers, fathers, sons and brothers, like the Ashbys for instance. It might also be noted how many of these joined the Royal Marines as Boy Buglers, which shows the influence they had in the Corps.

I was a member of a "family" in a way. The idea was, of course, as it was for many others, that my elder brother could "claim" me and we would serve together on the same ships. It was not long before I came to realize that maybe there were things I didn't want my brother to know about me and things he wouldn't want me to know about him, and he certainly wouldn't want me around his neck like a millstone, so we mutually agreed that we would go our own ways.

I think that at this time the authorities had the same idea, but for another reason. We were losing ships at an alarming rate, cruisers and even battleships, which sometimes meant the loss of father and son or brothers together. The sinking of HMS *Hood* brought this to mind in a dreadful way: of the nearly 1,200 men who were lost, most of them came from one division, Portsmouth, and many of them lived in the same area. Thereafter, although the Navy did not ban this "claiming", I don't think they encouraged it either, and they realized that the divisional system (Chatham, Portsmouth and Plymouth) posed a problem, with large numbers of local men all serving together and the possibility that a whole area might lose its menfolk in one go. I suspect that this in part caused the eventual break-up of the divisional system.

A Time for Reflection

Although I had attended school as required by law from the age of five onwards, I realize now that my education really started on that day when I entered Eastney Barracks, room B2 Band and Drums. I was on my own, or so I thought, no Mum or Dad, but I had just joined another family, which I was soon to recognize.

After all the boys had disappeared on their numerous duties at 8 a.m. on day one, I was on my own and began to think of what I had done when I had accepted the King's shilling. I had sworn to serve King and Country for twelve years from the age of eighteen, so I was going to serve four years for free before I even started my twelve-year engagement, and this for the princely sum of 1s. a day, which in these days of decimal coinage equals 36p a week.[1]

There were ways to scrounge things like forbidden cigarettes. One was to stand outside the "wet canteen" (the beer canteen which we were not allowed inside, of

---

[1] The decimal equivalents given for old currency do not take into account inflation.

course) and, with a penny in hand, approach the trained Marines and say "sell us a fag for a penny"; most took pity and gave it to us without taking the penny, sometimes you could get ten fags before someone eventually took it. My new family had started to educate me, and I would say that within three weeks I was as streetwise as any of Fagin's pupils.

When we did eventually "pass out" in 1939 our pay rose to 8s 9d (45p) a week and we could really lord it up. By then the realization had begun to dawn that life was not going to be as I had imagined it; the first survivors (boys) from ships sunk at sea had started to arrive back in barracks with their stories and I was on the verge of going to my first ship.

Day One

My mother's voice would gently call me, "Breakfast will be ready soon"; I would gradually realize that another day was about to start and swing my legs out of a soft, warm bed — alas, it was not to be on day one. I had not slept all that well, the night noises were something I had not heard before and, frankly, I was a bit shocked. Sleeping on a straw-filled palliasse was like lying on the back of a hedgehog. But nothing had prepared me for day one.

The bugler of the guard (something that I had to do eventually) blew "Reveille" at precisely the moment that the barracks clock struck 6 a.m. right outside one of our windows. There were no tannoy systems in those days and every command made to the barracks was by bugle. At 6 a.m. and thirty seconds someone entered the door and loudly proclaimed, "Out, out, out" and proceeded to tip each bed on to the floor. There was no special treatment for the new boy and I was told that I had fifteen minutes in which to fold the palliasse in half, strap it to the back of the bed, fold the blankets "like this", white, sheet, white, wrap the brown lengthwise around them and place on top of the folded palliasse, push the bottom half of the bed under the top, and then stand by it.

The floor of the room was covered in corticene, which was like a cork lino; this now had to be polished. Every one of the boys in the room was allocated a chore — clean fireplace and whiten it, chain polish the coal "bunce", clean the windows and, of course, polish the floor (the new boy joined that gang). About fifteen little lads were lined up in a row and given a piece of old blanket, then someone went in front of them with a spoon and delivered dollops of red polish on the floor, then it would start, rhythmically, left, right, left, right, all the way down the room and turn around and do the same on the way back. The cloths were replaced with clean pieces and the process was done all over again until that floor shone like a mirror — it was polished to such a degree that Torvill and Dean would have been delighted with it.

This was all done by 6.45 a.m., then you grabbed your towel and rushed over to the wash house for a very cold water wash and tooth clean, to be back by 7 a.m. for breakfast, the culinary excellence of which is worth another story. Then breakfast had to be eaten, buttons cleaned, badges polished, boots cleaned — all these hundred and one jobs had to be done to be on parade for 8 a.m. Of course, I hadn't got a uniform yet, this was going to be the day I was to be issued with all my bits and pieces, and the 8 o'clock parade could manage without me today; so all I could do was sit on my bed and watch, not

14

understanding anything that was going on. This was not a bit like yesterday, but my learning curve had begun, my first lesson being SURVIVE SOMEHOW.

Bedstraw

Having mentioned that palliasses had to be folded in half and strapped to the back of our bed irons, maybe I should explain more about this rather obscure item of bedding.

As I have said, a palliasse is a straw mattress and that, I can confirm, is exactly what it is, or was — a load of straw in a white mattress tick; that was our bed in the days before horse hair, "latex rubber biscuits" or feathers. The mattress itself was laid on "bed irons", two iron frames each with iron slats that could be slid one under the other to halve the space taken up each morning, and the palliasse was folded in half and strapped with a long piece of leather to the back end of the bed irons. The legs were secured to the bed by tapered cotter pins and it was always advisable to inspect these before sitting or lying on your bed, which was not allowed to be made until after 7p.m., as some joker would remove the cotter pins from the legs and the bed would collapse in a most untidy heap to the merriment of all those who were waiting for it to happen. However, we soon learnt not to do this to the "old soldiers" or the Corporal as they were apt to return from the local hostelry or wet canteen in not too jovial a mood, and to climb into a bed which collapsed called for retribution whereby everyone would finish up on the floor.

The life of a palliasse was about two months as I recall, during which time it had been lain on, sat on, jumped on and folded double every day which meant that the straw gradually broke down into chaff and dust and sleeping became very uncomfortable. Each room throughout the barracks was allocated a morning for everyone to refill their mattresses at the hay loft. As the number of rooms in the barracks was over the 100 mark, this must have been as unending a task as the painting of the Forth Bridge. Where all the straw came from, I hate to imagine; the horses had obviously finished with it for us to have it and I'm sure it was still warm sometimes.

The art of filling a mattress was to work in pairs, bearing in mind that the straw had to last for two months' severe treatment, so the idea was to get as much straw as possible into the mattress cover; you would push the straw in whilst your mate used his feet to pack it in good and firm until you had a tightly filled mattress which was completely round. This of course was very difficult to sleep on initially and even more difficult to fold in half each morning — it took at least a week to achieve something both comfortable and manageable.

I wondered sometimes if there were any small creatures left in the straw; I'm sure it wasn't disinfected in the hay loft, it seemed to be clean, but any bug that chose to live in a room full of drummers and buglers would have been crazy. I remember that mattress-filling day was full of laughter; we found ways of having fun in each other's company. It was called camaraderie.

My Debut

The first time Mum and Dad said they would come down to Eastney to see me filled me with excitement. I knew they would feed me and make me financially sound for a short while and, of course, I could show off in my new uniform. I suppose it was a month after I had arrived but it had taken at least three weeks to assemble all my kit. The accoutrements were no problem but the uniform had to be specially made, after all at 4' 8" I was not exactly off the peg, besides which we had to be trained in how to comport ourselves when out of barracks. In those days, when a Royal Marine went out he wore white cotton gloves and carried a silver-headed cane, something I was sorry to see discontinued as it made you feel a little special; but there was a drill to it all that had to be learnt before you were allowed out.

It was a Sunday, as I remember, and they would meet me at the barrack gate at 2p.m. by which time I had cleaned my buttons, boned my boots to the best possible shine for a new pair and starched my cap cover. We never had white-top caps then, just blue caps, but we donned cap covers between 1 May and 1

October and they had to be starched. A word about my boots; they too had to be made, by the cobblers in the barracks, from greased cow hide that took weeks and weeks of boning before getting the required polish. They were size six and each boot had 116 hobnails, a heel plate and a large toe plate; when I first put them on I felt like a deep-sea diver.

Two o'clock came eventually. I left it for a few minutes to make sure they would be there to see me march up to the Sergeant on the gate, and there they were, in earnest conversation with the Sergeant. Drawing myself up to my full height, I halted in front of the Sergeant.

"Po/x 3943 Boy Bugler L. Chester, permission to leave barracks, Sergeant."

My father was bursting with pride and my mother had tears in her eyes; I was terrified. Whilst I stood there with my proud parents watching, he did a 360-degree inspection of me, including a bird's eye view of my cap cover, because I'm sure he was 7' 6" tall.

"You have dust in the welts of your boots, go back and clean them properly."

My father's pride at that moment knew no bounds, my mother shed some more tears and I was completely humiliated. I have said that after three weeks we were completely streetwise, we had ways and means for all situations. For this one I went back to my barrack room, sat on the bed for ten minutes then walked back again.

"Why didn't you clean them like that the first time, laddie?"

In those halcyon pre-World War Two days, I'm sure that was the way of the Royal Marines, more so with the recruits: they endeavoured to break your spirit and then proceeded to build you up to what they wanted — sheer blind obedience. It worked, unless you were as cunning as us boys who had nothing to break down in the first place.

Name that Tune!

Someone once asked me, how did you buglers ever remember all those bugle calls? There were a lot of them and we had the worst of two worlds, all the Army calls and also those applicable to the Navy. I believe there were about 150 in total and, together with the ones for the drum and the flute, they were taught within six months. In October 1939 I "passed out" in front of Lieutenant Vivian Dunn as proficient on bugle, drum and flute, without being able to read a single note of music, thereby earning another 1s 9d (9p) a week.

Well, you don't always remember, but that comes later, it was easy really — we gave them all one common denominator, profanity, the more profane the words the easier they were to commit to memory. I can still recall the worst ones now, sixty-seven years later, so it must have worked well. As an example here is a clean one, it's "Mail Call" —

"A letter from Lousy Lou boys,
A letter from Lousy Lou."

Remember that and the tune sticks with it.

On the other hand, another method was used. I could never master the "First Mess" beatings on a drum. I was a "thicko" really, so the Bugle Major (a kindly man) stood behind me with a bass drum stick and repeatedly beat them out on my shoulders until they had sunk in; unfortunately the RM numerals on my shoulder epaulettes sunk into my shoulders as well and had to be dug out later. I can remember that drum beat to this day, so it must have worked. What a shame that we never had personal injury lawyers in those days.

One occasion when my memory did fail me was in January 1940. I had joined HMS *Iron Duke* on the Saturday and on the Sunday morning I was told to report to Jimmy the One for instructions for Sunday divisions. Who was Jimmy the One I asked, having been told that he was the Executive Officer. I eventually found him and he instructed me (after he had stopped laughing at the sight of me) to sound divisions in the port waist at 0.900 hours.

The time got nearer and nearer to 0.900 hours and I still had no idea who, what or where the port waist was, so I thought I must swallow my pride and ask this nice sailor, which I did.

"Yer innit," he said with all the grace of an Elizabethan pirate.

When the divisions had all been mustered in their different parts of the ship, the Captain said to me,

"Bugler, sound the 'Close Aft for Prayers'."

A simple call, easily remembered, but at that moment I knew exactly how Sir Laurence Olivier would have felt if he had forgotten the opening lines to *Hamlet*, sheer naked panic and terror. The Captain could see that there was no way his bugler was going to remember "Close Aft" so, calling over the Sergeant-Major of Marines, in front of everyone mustered on the quarterdeck he said, "March this bloody bugler away and bring him back when he can remember the 'Close Aft'."

I suppose there have been worse musical debuts but I have never forgotten that bugle call even to this day. That was another way of learning.

I had the last laugh in a sense, though. As we went to "Air Raid Warning Red" I remembered the "Alarm to Arms — Repel Boarders", but a German dropped a bomb on us which served that Captain right because it blew a ruddy great hole in the ship's side. It didn't pay to upset a Royal Marine bugler, we had powerful friends.

The Sick, the Lame
and the Weary

It may be that my memory is at fault — after all, many
years have gone by — but for the life of me I cannot
recall any of the thirty Boy Buglers in our barrack room
ever catching a cold or going down with flu, and it was
as prevalent then as it is today. Mind you, it was just as
well it would not have done you any good if you had
caught a cold or flu, for sympathy and compassion were
in very short supply. You would not be told to stay in
bed whither someone would bring hot lemon or a hot
water bottle. If you were breathing then you were fit to
get on parade and do drill, bugle, flute and drum
practice along with everyone else; if you had stopped
breathing you would be told to report to the office for
sick parade.

"Sick Call" was always sounded fifteen minutes
before the main parade formed up, and you would then
muster with all the other "SL&W" (sick, lame and
weary) in the covered drill shed and march to the
infirmary. Woe betide any of the older hands who had
been to sea calling it the sick bay. "We don't want any

of your sea language here, boy, it's the infirmary", and never mind if you were out on your feet or had ingrowing toenails, you marched the three-quarters of a mile to the infirmary. There was then a very long wait in a cold stone waiting room until the naval doctor arrived, who would examine you and pronounce whether you were sick or fit for duty. If you were unfit for duty but not a "bedcase" you would be placed on "light duty", whereby you remained in the infirmary, not resting though, but working like a slave cleaning the wards etc. and returning to the barrack room at the end of the day. This would be repeated ad infinitum until you were once again declared fit for duty.

I can only remember two occasions when I went "sick". Once I had a bad reaction to one of the numerous vaccinations and was ill with "vaccinitis" and put to bed in the infirmary. I didn't stay very long: the first enema administered by an enormous matron seemed to cure me very quickly, anything was better; than that affront to one's dignity. The other occasion occurred after I had paid a visit to the naval dentist for a filling. It was the first time in my life that I had cocaine injections for fillings and on the way back to barracks with a completely numb mouth I thought, how wonderful — but somehow I managed to bite through my top inside lip, quite badly as well, which developed into a large hole. I showed this to the Bugle Major and explained that no way could I blow a bugle with a mouth like that, but he said, "Take no notice of it, boy, blow with it, it will make your lips tougher". I still have a faint scar in the middle of my top lip.

Like I said, sympathy and compassion were in very short supply. I was only pleased that I never caught flu, which could have entailed a lengthy stay in the infirmary — that matron had the largest fingers I have ever seen!

The First Signs of War

I know that World War Two was declared on 3 September 1939, but for me the first signs that war had started became apparent in June 1939. The government had at last decided to call up all reservists, so it seemed that conflict was now inevitable and would only be a matter of time, or a cinder to start the fire. We had of course been girding our loins ready for battle for some time; Boy Buglers we may have been, but we were a vital cog in the war machine.

The day of mobilization came and Eastney Barracks prepared for the great influx of reservists coming in answer to the call of Drake's Drum. The drill shed had been made into an enormous reception and registration station lined with tables labelled alphabetically and manned by a Sergeant, an Officer and a Boy Bugler to act as messenger and general "gopher". I had been allocated to table D. We went into action very early in the day, as was the usual practice, ready for the flood of men streaming in to do their duty to King and Country. We could have had a lie-in as nobody came other than a few dribs and drabs, nothing to alarm the Germans. Very disappointing really — all those reservists had been paid about 1s a week and taken to camp in the summer each year and now it seemed they didn't want to come back for a war; that was gratitude for you.

I can remember our Officer saying to the Sergeant (he wouldn't have deigned to include me in the conversation), "they won't be coming in until the public houses close". I can imagine that "Charlie Hurdles" (the Cumberland Arms to the uninitiated) would have been doing a very brisk trade. How right he was for once, for as soon as the last orders had been supped they staggered in, in droves and in all stages of inebriation; the majority couldn't even find the right desk, it was pure pantomime.

My one lasting memory, though, was that amongst the throng, here and there were men still wearing a "Broderick", some even with a Royal Marine Light Infantry cap badge, and they had disappeared in 1923. The Broderick was similar to the peaked cap worn today except that it had no peak and had a half-moon red flash together with the cap badge. To my young eyes these men were grandfathers — they weren't of course — it was just that men seemed to age prematurely then. They were all absorbed into the barracks one way or another. These were the men who took us into the early days of World War Two.

The Day War Broke Out

The day that World War Two broke out is vivid in my memory, not because it was a momentous occasion, but because Hitler really did annoy Herbie Tydd and me that day.

It was a Sunday of course and Sunday means Church Parade; anyone who can remember those halcyon days before the war in the vicinity of Eastney Barracks will know that Church Parade was quite a spectacle. The parade ground would be full of Marines and the band would be in full ceremonial dress ready to march the parade to St Andrew's Church and, after the church service, march the parade back again, by which time the local populace was allowed in to see the band perform. Herbie and I had been detailed for the band that day; it was our first day in dress uniform. I was in the second row of drums whilst Herbie, who was the Drum Major's blue-eyed boy, was on tenor drums. That was a particular honour as you got to wear the leopard skin and white gauntlets and were able to perform all manner of dextrous movements with the drum sticks — and you had to be an expert to do that. So there we stood, full dress uniform, regimental drums, silver bugles and white helmets, ready for our debut before an audience.

We were in church and about halfway through the service when an orderly marched up the aisle and whispered to the padre, who then announced "We are now at war with Germany" and in the circumstances we should all make our way quietly back to barracks and await further orders. So we never did get to perform in full regalia before an adoring public. The disappointment and chagrin were awful and Herbie and I never forgave Hitler for that. Couldn't Mr Chamberlain have waited just another two hours until Church Parade was finished?

Later that day we received our first wartime directive and it was "to drown all cats". We had two in our block and the tabby had just had kittens; they had to be drowned though, orders is orders. I have never understood that instruction but I think the powers that be thought that we were destined for immediate air raids and they didn't want rabid cats everywhere. I don't know if that was the true reason but the war was very odd at times

B-flat Low-pitched Flute

Not only did we, as Boy Buglers, have to learn the 150 or so bugle calls and their variations, together with all the intricacies of drum work and stick movements (not all of it to do with marching with the band as some orders were still given by the drum), but we also had to learn how to play a B-flat low-pitched flute and this meant the worst lessons of all, flute practice each night at 7p.m. I found learning music absolute purgatory, I don't think I ever did master the difference between a minim and a quaver and never in my life have I ever been able to read a note of music. Yet within weeks of having been fitted out with a uniform we had to take our place in the drum and flute band every Saturday morning parade, the main band having a day off on Saturday. We felt very important with a music lyre strapped on the left wrist to hold the music card, marching along pretending to blow a flute and reading the music on the card — all completely superfluous of course as the senior boys were the source of the music, we were only there to make up the numbers.

But flute practice was agony, a dozen boys sat down at a long table being taught the notes on a flute and the scales with an instructor Corporal walking behind armed with a dress cane waiting to catch someone fingering a wrong note; if you were quick, you could move your fingers away before the cane arrived. Despite all this, though, within six months I was ready to go before a Board having learnt the bugle calls, drum beats and two marches on a flute — and me without the slightest knowledge of a note of music. My friend Podge delighted in telling how, when it came to the flute marches, he copied the fingering of the boy in front and scraped through with a "Superior" whilst the other boy only had a "Satisfactory".

When we had satisfied the Board that we were competent on all three we were "passed for duty", so their methods of teaching must have had some effect. We were now allowed to wear tassels on our bugle strings and dress tassels on our uniform on all formal occasions, and our pay went up, as I have mentioned. It also meant that we were now available to be sent wherever we were required to go. Our war had started.

Pay Books

In about March/April 1940 we were informed that everybody was to be issued with a pay book, therefore we would all have to have our photos taken as mugshots to be stuck inside. The pay book would contain everything that anyone needed to know about you — credentials, rate of pay, increments earned, distinguishing marks, next of kin, etc. It would be more detailed than a passport. Because of this it had to be kept on your person at all times and never ever let out of sight; to lose it was a very serious offence indeed. It was said that if a fifth columnist obtained one, then a spy could assume your identity with complete ease — that is why it was such an important booklet. If at any time we happened to be stopped by Redcap Military Police, the first thing we were asked for was our pay book, which would tell them all they wanted to know about us.

So everyone on the ship had to file on to the quarter-deck, where a photographer was waiting. When I reached the age of eighteen I was no longer classed as a boy, I was now a man, but of course my looks had changed (I was much more handsome, even though I say so myself), so it entailed having a new photo done. Somehow I must have persuaded someone to let me keep the old one, which had been taken when I was fourteen; it is a little tattered and torn, but after all it is sixty-seven years old. It's amazing that it has lasted through the years.

Old Sweats

It's remarkable, when one reflects on the years before the war, how different life was and how one's perception of all things has changed — dare I say, not always for the best. I remember thinking, as a boy in the Royal Marines, how old everyone seemed. I was seeing them through the eyes of a fourteen-year-old of course, but an "old sweat" who had three good conduct badges and had not yet gone to pension could only have been thirty-nine years old at most if he had joined at eighteen and yet he was an old man to me.

The barracks was full of these "old sweats" before the war, each with his own comfortable little niche which he had reckoned on staying in until the day he went to pension. We called them "barrack stanchions" and it was said unkindly, as they stayed behind whilst everyone else went to sea. There were, of course, a hundred and one jobs within the barracks that required these stanchions and really they were the men who made everyday life run as smoothly as it did. The tailors, not a recognized trade, who could sit on a table top cross-legged like so many elves — try it, it is not easy. The boot makers, or "snobs", the barbers, the ground keepers, the gardeners, the Officers' mess waiters, the type cutters. Everyone had to have a wooden type with which to mark their kit, it had the name on one side and the regimental number on the other, and these were carved by hand from a piece of beech wood at the cost of 1d a letter — alright for Cox but costly for Oswaldthistlewaite. Every department, office, store and barrack room had its share of "old sweats".

Declaration of World War Two brought this to an abrupt end. All these "stanchions" had skills that were now needed as ships' complements were to be brought up to wartime levels and a new breed was a-coming in, "HOs", hostilities-only men who were being called up for the duration of the war, men who had civilian skills which fitted into the gap admirably. If you had worked for Burton's, the clothing store awaited; if for David Griegs, into the ration store. Barbers, bricklayers, tailors, plumbers, all were received with open arms and found niches which lasted throughout the war. Not that that happened to them all — the majority served in wartime conditions the same as the rest of us.

So the war was to go on for six years to its ultimate ending; then the "HOs" wanted out, to get back to their families and resume their lives, but within the Corps no one had been trained for these jobs any longer and new blood had joined, the "old sweats" had gone. The Royal Marines faced a difficult time and there was even talk of disbandment; but then along came the Commandos and they saved the Corps and made it what it is today. But it isn't the regiment I knew as a boy. When the

Marines were first formed in 1664 they were known as The Duke of York and Albany's Maritime Regiment of Foot; they have changed, that's progress.

Pay

As I have said, we were paid 1s. a day. But out of this grand sum 1s 9d was deducted and placed into an account to be paid when you attained the age of eighteen, so in fact we only drew 5s 3d (26p) a week, out of which we had to buy all our everyday requirements — soap, toothpaste, Bluebell, boot polish and so on. Yet somehow we always seemed to finish with enough for pictures on a Saturday afternoon and half a pound of angel cake to take back for a feast in the evening — we were always hungry.

There were alternative ways of getting things like forbidden "fags", you could always beg; but our skills were in scrounging, we became past masters at this as we became streetwise. The Artful Dodger would have lost the coat off his back within ten minutes in our room. I have mentioned before how we would wait outside the beer canteen (we weren't allowed in of course), and with a penny in hand and a doleful face we would approach some Marine and say "Sell us a fag for a penny".

In barracks Royal Marines came under the Army Act, but once on board ship we came under the

Admiralty and Admiralty Fleet Orders, so we boys were paid the same as Royal Navy boys, 6s (30p) a fortnight; the remainder went into your "account". But even then we managed to exist and smoked like chimneys with tobacco costing 1s 9d a pound and we could always sell any excess. Many boys took up skills like haircutting, snobbing boots or tailoring, talents that had no recognized trade in the Services; but the boy who was the only one on a ship who could cut hair was maybe on his way to being a millionaire next year.

My other bugler, Curly Regan, and I had a "dhobi" firm and as we lived in with the band on HMS *King George V* we had a constant demand for clean laundry, starched shorts and shirts every day. How we managed this when we had no electric irons remains our secret, but it was a lovely little earner!

When we eventually "passed out" as competent buglers, drummers and flautists our pay rose to 8s 9d (45p) a week, as I have said, and we could really lord it up then.

My eighteenth birthday, my rainy day, did come — it must have done — although I can't remember it. It would have been on 5 April 1943 whilst I was in the Mediterranean and probably went on wine, women, and song. Why leave it to earn interest; there were men out there trying to kill us and they were very good at it too.

My Friend

We were always grateful for having a friend like Hodge. He was Hodge in those days of our youth; it wasn't until later years when he was older and more rotund that someone remarked, "He ain't Hodge, he's Podge," and so the name stuck. He didn't do us any favours or anything like that, but he had one advantage that none of us others had: his mother was a cook in the cookhouse and not, I may add, a person to be trifled with.

Naturally, with this attribute it was always Hodge who was sent to collect our food from the cookhouse. As I have mentioned, we didn't have such a luxury as a mess hall or communal cafeteria; we all ate in our barrack rooms and the food had to be collected from the cook-house in trays and then dished out when it subsequently arrived, mostly cold, wet if it was raining. I'm sure the inmates of Alcatraz dined better than we did. The trestle tables in the barrack room were used for drum practice when the weather was wet and for flute practice every evening. It was quite a distance to the cookhouse to collect our trays and the tea was made in large stainless steel tea urns; as we only had little legs it used to slop down us.

Here of course is where Hodge's mum comes into the picture. She was ever eager to look after her Harold and took pity on all the other hungry boys as well; we never had enough food and we were all growing lads, so mum always used to put a bit extra in our trays — sometimes we got two sausages instead of one and heaps of mashed potatoes. It was always so whenever we sent Hodge to collect our food.

When World War Two was declared things had to change; spare barrack rooms were required for the influx of men coming in, so by the time I returned to barracks in 1942 a general mess hall had been built and Hodge's mum had been co-opted into the WRNS and was now Wren Overbury, with an oversized blue uniform and a sailor's hat — quite fetching.

Podge's Mum

To illustrate the remark I made that Wren Overbury was not to be trifled with, I will relate the tale of the complaint. It must have been sometime in 1942 when it happened as I had just returned to barracks after two years on my first ship and the new mess hall had been built.

We had liver and onions for breakfast, "baby's head and guardrails" as it was known in the vernacular. The liver was like the soles of our boots and the onions looked like bootlaces, most unappetizing. In comes the Officer of the day, as was his duty at every meal, being concerned about our well-being.

"Any complaints?" he asks, holding his nose twixt finger and thumb.

"Yes," says Hodge.

Well, you may have seen a cartoon where the Officer is aghast and the Corporal swells with indignation; this is where it originated.

"Taste this liver and onions, sir, we can't eat it and we are told we must have a good breakfast before going on parade."

"Don't talk to the Officer like that, son," says the Corporal.

Mind you, the Officer had to agree that it was pretty gruesome and he was due for his own breakfast shortly.

"Fetch this man another breakfast."

Up comes a plate with egg, bacon and fried bread.

"Do you withdraw your complaint?"

"Yes, sir," says Hodge.

On the way to the washing-up space, in a corridor, he is suddenly grabbed by a huge Sergeant in cook's whites and literally lifted off the floor by his neck.

"Are you the little . . . who just made the complaint?"

"Yes, Sergeant," squeaks Hodge.

"Do you realize that it was my breakfast that you have just eaten?"

"No," says Hodge, "and if you don't put me down I shall report you."

"Who the hell do you think you are?" says Sergeant.

"I'm Po/x3834 Boy Bugler Harold Overbury."

At this the Sergeant turns a paler shade of pale.

"Is Mrs Overbury your mum?" he asks in a squeaky voice.

"Yes," says Hodge.

"God, you won't tell her, will you?" he says, and gently lowers Hodge to the ground, straightening his tunic and dusting him down.

As far as I can remember, Hodge never had reason to complain henceforth — that was the kind of fear Hodge's mum could instil. Bombs, bullets, even a draft to a ship were not equal to the wrath of Mrs Overbury protecting her young.

Going to War

Once a Boy Bugler had "passed for duty" he became available for drafting to ships etc. I have stressed the nomenclature of Boy Bugler because we remained as such until the age of eighteen when we had the choice of remaining a bugler or transferring to the ranks and becoming a fully trained Marine, which was the option most of us went for.

When I passed for duty I was not yet fifteen, but my time had come to join the battle against the Hun. I never fully understood how the drafting system worked; I know it was all done from PRORM (Pay and Records Office Royal Marines) which was at Chatham, but did they designate who should go where, or did they just apply for a certain required number of bodies and leave it up to the local barracks to designate who went where?

Whichever, there always seemed to be an element of favouritism in it somewhere. I know of many boys who went to active sea-going ships, whilst others went to naval establishments and were on shore all the time they served as Boy Buglers, never going to sea all through the war — places like the Naval Barracks or

HMS *Royal Arthur*, which was the former Billy Butlin's holiday camp at Skegness, some of which were near enough for them to be able to go home on frequent occasions. But others went to ships and died on them, like Froggie French and Peter Avant on HMS *Fiji*. There were two Boy Buglers serving on every ship, from cruisers upwards, that was lost at sea; not all of them died, many survived, but they were soon returned to another ship.

I was sent to HMS *Iron Duke*, something between the two.

Why Didn't I Look Where
I Was Going?

So there I was, travelling with a detachment of thirty Marines for my first posting to a battleship.

There were two train routes to Scrabster, which is the penultimate stop for Scapa Flow and the harbour where the ferry boat takes over. Thurso is the end of the line as far as the railway goes and, having got there, you will have travelled the length of the British Isles; going any further would mean getting your feet wet. From Euston you go up the western route as far as Carlisle, then across to Inverness, where it converges with the eastern route from King's Cross via York and Edinburgh; from Inverness onwards it is single-line to Thurso if you are lucky. I say that because the line to Thurso wends its way through the most spectacular and remote of the Scottish Highlands, the Western Highlands, and in the winter it is invariably snowbound, which at times has meant a stay in Inverness until the line was opened.

I have done that journey many times one way or another and yet not once did I bother to look at what I was missing out of the window; the whole journey was a nuisance to be suffered until the destination was reached, whether it was London or Thurso. Never did I ever appreciate the privilege I was being given of doing a trip that I would now give my eye teeth for and which would make a severe dent in my bank balance — and all for free. It should have been a journey of sheer delight and interest, instead of which the men in the carriage would gather as much beer as possible and arrive at Thurso or London with a massive hangover. Not that I was old enough to partake of the beer — I was small enough (I was now 4′ 10″) to be placed up in the luggage rack to sleep most of the way. I have to say that this mode of travel was uncomfortable but sleep was a way of ignoring the fact that we had no food, and I most certainly didn't have enough money to buy any.

The journey down to London was the worst, no food and no water — that is why they stocked up with beer. I have known that journey to take twenty-nine hours; we nearly always arrived during an air raid which meant that the train slowed to almost walking pace from Watford Junction to London in case of any unseen damage to the railway line. Going back after leave was a bit better as Mother would "do me up" some sandwiches, and — God bless them, for ever after I have put money in their boxes — the Salvation Army came to our rescue. At Brora, well up in the Highlands and on the last leg to Thurso, an extra coach was joined on to the train from which the Sally Army dispensed soya links and mash free of charge to all the servicemen on board. I have never forgotten that.

Having arrived at Thurso all men going to Scapa Flow were bussed to Scrabster to board the *St Ninian*, the ferry boat, a tall, single-funnelled 1,000-ton old rusty sick bucket that would take us over the Pentland Firth to Scapa Flow. We who had done the trip many times knew what to do, but the novices all rushed below to occupy the few bunks available, poor fools; we bedded down on the lee (sheltered) side, by the warm funnel in the fresh air. The Pentland Firth is renowned as the worst stretch of water in the British Isles; on one side the Atlantic, on the other the North Sea, and the tide race between the two is phenomenal. A swimmer would not survive in it to be sure. The old *St Ninian* would twist this way and that way, up and down; below decks where the bunks were it was pitiful, the stench was awful and the sea sick would be slopping from one side to the other.

I've seen men praying for a torpedo to end their misery, but the Germans never wanted to waste a torpedo on the *St Ninian*, which they must have spotted many times — in fact I heard that they once volunteered to tow her into Scapa Flow.

A Change of Scenery

Life aboard HMS *Iron Duke*, which I shall also refer to as the "Tin Duck", was not easy, I can vouch for that. My first impression on climbing the gangway to the quarterdeck the day I joined her was the all-pervading stench of oil. I suppose we got used to it after a while but even to this day the smell of a hot car engine with its whiff of oil will arouse something in the back of my memory.

I had left behind all those other lads in room B2 who had become my family and here I was, the only fourteen-year-old among a thousand men; the other bugler, Gibson, was about sixteen and had joined up at a later age, but we were both as green as grass and knew not which was the sharp end or the blunt end. One has to understand that the peacetime Navy still reigned, regulations were not as relaxed as they were to be later in the war, and one of the rules was that boys were not allowed to fraternize with men and vice versa — we were not permitted to talk with them officially unless it was in the course of our duty. Paedophiles are not something new, they have always been around and I had to be protected from their attentions. Talk to any old Navy hand and he will tell you that the Navy was run on "rum, bum and baccy".

This protection was so severe that I had to lead an almost monastic life of silence. I was not allowed to linger on the Royal Marines' mess deck and had to live in the Sergeants' mess, where I became an unpaid skivvy to fetch and serve. Ironically, it was in the Sergeants' mess that I got the most sexual innuendoes. One particular Sergeant whenever he saw me used to sing a little ditty —

"Sticky red, sticky blue,
Here's a fathom up your flue"

(all drummers were called "sticks", by the way) — he thought it ever so funny. I met him a few years later when he was a patient of Dr McIndoe's for plastic surgery; his face was unrecognizable having been burnt aboard an aircraft carrier in the Mediterranean during an air raid.

But it was here that I was thrown close to the Sergeants' messman, an old three-badge Marine named "Lofty" Dewey, who was 6′ 6″ if he was an inch and was approaching pension age but would be retained for the duration of the war. He became my mentor, tutor and protector without asking anything in return and without him I don't think I would have survived.

At night I had to sling my hammock outside the Captain's cabin, not only for protection but to be available to the Captain if there was an air raid or some other emergency; there wasn't a broadcasting system installed so my bugle was what conveyed all instructions.

The compartment (called a "flat") where the Captain had his cabin was right in the stern of the ship, beneath the quarterdeck, not very spacious; and at the other end of the flat was a glass cabinet containing a dummy wearing the uniform of Admiral Jellicoe complete with a telescope under his arm. The "Tin Duck" had been his flagship at the Battle of Jutland, you see. This dummy used to give me nightmares; the flat would only be dimly lit with emergency lighting during the night and if I peeped over the side of my hammock I could see Admiral Jellicoe. I swear he used to walk about during the night. I suppose things were getting to me.

Lofty always used to say to me "never get yourself into a confined space with Marine XXXX", and except for one occasion I never did. I had been "naughty" and was up before the Captain of Marines actually on a charge of mutiny (see page 67). Part of my punishment was to clean out the baggage store which was where I got trapped by Marine XXXX, but by this time I was far too streetwise to get caught like that and escaped to safety.

We Boy Buglers were faced with this kind of sexual harassment and innuendo nearly every day of our lives in one way or another.

Call the Hands

Chippy Carpenter was an artist, there was no doubt about that; but to me he was a genius. I never did find out his age, he appeared to be as old as the hills whereas I was just turned fifteen. He was a chip off that Heart of Oak that made the Royal Navy long before World War Two, as we used to say when men were made of steel and ships of wood — not like today, when men are made of wood and ships of steel. I don't agree with that sentiment now, I have learnt many truths. Chippy was the Quartermaster of my watch and I was the Boy Bugler; we worked as a team did Chippy and I, in a ship which had no broadcasting system and which worked to the bugle and the pipe.

At 6a.m. it was our job to "Call the Hands", in landlubber's terms "Reveille", he with his pipe (bo'sun's call) and me with a bugle. I bugled and he piped on every mess deck throughout the ship, and having been all the way round once it was time to start off on the next call. No wonder buglers were nearly always small, they obviously used up all their energy. You had to have a masochistic streak in your character to open the watertight door to a mess deck, festooned with hammocks like so many bats in a belfry, poke a bugle in, take a deep breath and let them have "Reveille". I consoled myself with the thought that if I couldn't be asleep, why should anyone else.

When I had finished, Chippy would start his solo piece and I swear he could go from one end of the ship to the other and only repeat himself twice. His repertoire was endless and would begin,

"Wakey wakey, rise and shine,
Get out and put your hammocks in a line,
Let go of your xxxxs
And grab hold of your socks,
The sun's scorching your eyes out,
Kippers and custard for breakfast"

and so on, the rest being unprintable; but to our credit not many men were charged with being a "late hammock".

Sometimes I look back and think that I must have been one of the last buglers to sound calls like "Work Main Derrick" when coaling ship, or to make that trek all the way around a battleship, at "Air Raid Warning Red" I had to run round sounding "Action Stations"; if I was quick I could get back to the quarterdeck before the air raid was over. It was during one of those occasions when a German pilot tried to kill me. None of this was going to be required in the new ships coming into being, when I just stood alongside a broadcasting system and one bugle call sufficed.

I did hear of Chippy once more after the war, sometime in 1979 when I renewed the acquaintance of an author, Thurlow Craig, who had been an Officer on HMS *Iron Duke*. He even recalled me and said he had always kept in touch with Chippy, but Chippy had died. I was surprised really as Chippy was a character and as solid a seaman as they come. I thought he would go on for ever — but there, nothing ever does.

Scapa Flow: HMS Royal Oak

October 1939 was a disastrous month for Scapa Flow, the impregnable fortress and safe haven for the Royal Navy in the north, but mistakes were being made and unfortunately mistakes are never recognized until they have been made; the answer is to learn from them and take the necessary action to make sure they don't happen again. I have to say that the Royal Navy did this, and very quickly.

Much has already been written about what happened on the night of 14 October 1939 so I don't intend to go into it in detail, but U-47, captained by Günther Prien, certainly did get into the Flow at 23.30 hours. I spent two years in one spell in Scapa Flow and also made many subsequent visits during the course of World War Two, so I can safely say that Günther Prien, even with the aid of the Aurora Borealis, would have been able to see very little in the middle of an October night — it would have been darker than the inside of a witch's nightie.

The story as we old Scapa hands knew it was that he made out two dark shapes, one behind the other with one of them to the side. The nearest was HMS *Pegasus*, a World War One cruiser that had been converted into a seaplane carrier, quite an innovation in the days before the advent of modern aircraft carriers. The seaplanes would be craned over the side of the ship to take off and would then become the eyes of the fleet for eighty to a hundred miles, an advantage that was breathtaking in those early days. Behind HMS *Pegasus* lay HMS *Royal Oak*; both were in Kirkwall Bay, which is not the usual fleet anchorage but they were there to provide anti-aircraft cover for Kirkwall.

How naive we were. U-47 fired its first salvo of three torpedoes which were aimed at the first target; this would have been HMS *Pegasus*, but because she was of a very shallow draught they either missed altogether or passed underneath. But one of the torpedoes did hit the bows of HMS *Royal Oak*. It has never really been explained why the ship's company just felt a slight bump and failed to take due notice or alarm. Having seen ships torpedoed, this is unbelievable.

At 01.22 hours U-47 reloaded, fired a further spread of three torpedoes and then beat a hasty retreat out of the Flow whilst noting that this time they had found a mark. The torpedoes' strike was of course what sank the ship, but before she went down the explosion created what we now know as a "fire flash" which swept through the ship from one end to the other and is thought to have caused most of the 833 casualties. It was intensely hot, moving at the speed of an express train, and invisible; most men were still in their hammocks and never knew what happened. Topside, panic and disbelief reigned; no one thought that a submarine could be inside Scapa Flow and even the Court of Inquiry found it hard to accept.

Meanwhile, on board HMS *Iron Duke* anchored in Lyness Bay the other side of the Flow, little was heard; some said they could make out a dull thud but the first intimation that anything was wrong was when all boats were called away. The battleship had no tannoy system and so men slept on, only to be told next morning that HMS *Royal Oak* had been sunk within the Flow.

Mistakes had been made or maybe the Royal Navy, in all its arrogance, had never ever contemplated that the enemy would enter the Flow, but once the truth emerged they reacted very quickly and Scapa Flow was sealed against any further intruders, albeit too late for HMS *Royal Oak*.

I think I am correct in saying that the experience made the Navy "aware" of the fire flash because by April 1940 we were all issued with anti-flash equipment, headgear and arm-length gloves.

I have been back to Scapa Flow in recent years on other research, but whilst there I looked in the military cemetery in Lyness for the graves of two whom I knew. There are only twenty-six graves; where are the other 800 men? They are still inside the wreck — that is why it is a registered War Grave.

Scapa Flow:
My Name Wasn't On It

HMS *Royal Oak* was sunk on 14 October, but few may remember that we had an air raid on the Flow three days later by forty German bombers during which HMS *Iron Duke* was hit by a bomb on the port side midships; this made a hole in the ship's side large enough to drive a double-decker bus through. The immediate list caused such great concern that action had to taken quickly or we would suffer the loss of a second battleship in three days.

Two conditions were against her survival. Firstly she was an old World War One battleship dating from 1913, not built to withstand air attack and constructed before the advent of small watertight compartments; there were vast areas of open mess decks and passages and once flooding started there would be little hope of stopping it.

Secondly, like all the ships at anchor in this "phoney war" period, and as I mentioned earlier, she was at seven hours' notice for steam — that's how long it would take to get the ship under way, she didn't have a self-starter. Every available vessel was therefore utilized to tow her round to Melsetter Bay, opposite the village of Longhope from where she was anchored in Lyness Bay. Unfortunately for the crew, they could not have found a more isolated or desolate place to park her, not a building in sight, not a tree to be seen, just hills and open water and completely unprotected — as was obvious in the next air raid on 16 March 1940 when she was hit again, this time on the starboard side forward, which made another hole, but this time only capable of admitting a single-decker bus.

To make the occasion even more memorable, it was during this air raid that a stray German plane jettisoned its bomb on to a crofter's cottage at the Bridge of Wraithe at Stenness, killing a Mr Isbister and making him the first civilian to be killed by a German bomb on British soil — a notoriety that he never lived to enjoy. I was very lucky during that raid as I was sent with a message to the bomb area and had to move along the starboard waist when I heard the whine of a plane diving. I didn't wait but ran as fast as I could, easily breaking the four-minute mile, undoing eight cleats on an armoured door and getting inside to safety. The plane machine-gunned all down the starboard side and after the raid I dug a bullet out of the decking where, a short time before, I had run. I still have that bullet — it is a tracer bullet — but it hasn't got my name on it.

As Lord Haw-Haw used to announce in his broadcasts, "We know all about that citadel in the mud." Citadel indeed — she couldn't harm a fly if the Germans only knew it, her anti-aircraft protection was two 3-inch guns and a hastily mounted twin .303 Lewis gun, hardly anything to worry a German pilot. Those 3-inch guns were nasty weapons, though, to the men who manned them, not the enemy: I always blamed one for the loss of hearing in my right ear, as whilst an air raid was in progress I walked out of a screen door just beneath the gun when it was fired. The crack of that gun damaged my ear drums to this day.

Over the next few months, though, a few more guns like pom-poms and Oerlikons were installed and the old "Tin Duck" became an integral part of the famous Scapa Flow anti-aircraft "box", which was laughable really; but her starboard side 6-inch gun battery certainly covered Hoxa boom and she became a transit ship for men awaiting the return of a ship which may have been at sea.

She was never to sail the seas again. There she would remain beached and see out the remainder of World War Two until sometime in 1946 when she was towed away to be scrapped.

Scapa Flow:
The Beginning of Lyness

In those early days of the war in 1940, Scapa Flow was no place for a boy. There were no pubs, clubs, cinemas or trees and very little in the way of habitation, just green hills, sheep and foul weather. It was little surprise, therefore, that we had a fairly constant stream of straitjacketed patients going over to the hospital ship *Amarapoora*, never to be seen again. I've often wondered how I survived; I suppose at that age I must have thought that this was how life was, I had known little else.

In May 1940 we had a whole lot of Marines arrive on the "Tin Duck". We were told that they were fresh conscripts and had only been called up ten days previously, just long enough to be fitted with khaki battledress but not long enough for even one of them to possess a rifle. They were on their way to Namsos in Norway solely as a Pioneer Company, but of course by then we had begun to retreat from Norway, so they were held back. I recall them being lined up on deck and a Captain of

Marines walking along saying, "You, you and you Lance Corporals" and "You, you and you Corporals" with a Sergeant-Major taking down the names of his newly promoted NCOs. I remember his name — it was Philpotts — and by a sheer quirk of coincidence his son, who was also a Royal Marine in his time, lived in Tavistock, where I live at the moment. He died two years ago at the age of eighty-two and I used to take great pleasure in telling him how I served with his father.

As there was no point in the Company going to Norway now, and they couldn't stay on the "Tin Duck", what was to be done? They were sent round to the port of Lyness where they were put under canvas, and it became like a Wild West town that the miners lived in on their way to Alaska, tents, mud and duckboards — if you stepped from them the chances were that you were never seen again. I remember vividly watching the film *Pinocchio* in a small tent, after which everyone retired to the beer tent for their coupon allocation of beer, which — as there were no glasses available — was drunk from enamelled mugs. This was not for me, though — the mere smell of the tent made me dizzy — so I did not go ashore very often as it was our only place of liberty; the fleet canteen on the island of Flotta had not yet been built.

The Marines who had been dumped in Lyness eventually built it into a town, as they comprised men of every trade and skill; I have read that at one time there were 6,000 men and women based there and it

Scapa Flow:
A Casual Stroll

There were no distractions for me in Scapa Flow; therefore at one period, other than home leave once a year, I never set foot on dry land or left the ship.

Somehow this was brought to the attention of the ship's Captain, a Commander Boutwood, who incidentally did all the diving on the *Royal Oak* and later became Captain of HMS *Curacoa*, which was cut in half in a collision with the *Queen Mary* in 1942 with the loss of most of the ship's company. Noting that I had not been ashore, he ordered that the Sergeant-Major was to take me for a route march. I could see that he was not pleased with that order; I could tell by his manner that his attitude was "I'll make this little sod suffer", and in a way he did. On board ship we didn't wear the hobnailed boots we wore whilst in barracks, we wore sea service boots, soft normal boots with leather soles which wouldn't tear the wooden decks to pieces; so for my solitary route march I was made to wear my shore service boots, and off we went for our enjoyable stroll.

I'm sure we walked (or marched) ten miles. But of course here I had a problem: I was a growing lad and, as I had been away for about eighteen months, my feet had developed in proportion to other parts of my body; my boots were size six but my feet were now a gigantic size seven. So what started off as a pleasant walk ended in agony and when we at last got into the pinnace that was sent for us at Longhope, I just dunked boots and feet into the water midst a cloud of steam. When I took off my boots my greyback socks were red with blood and in the ensuing days I lost both toenails off my big toes.

It was an interesting walk, though. I even got to see the Old Man of Hoy — and don't take that the wrong way.

Scapa Flow:
Mutiny!

In a previous story I mentioned that I had been "naughty" and was on a charge of mutiny so I feel I should tell more about this as it sounds dreadful and at the time, for me, it was. I had visions of being keelhauled or some such awful fate.

It was the duty of the bugler of the forenoon watch to clean the ship's bell and on the *Iron Duke* it was an enormous great thing that I am sure could be heard all over the Flow. On this particular morning, a Sunday, I was on watch in what was known as No. 3 dress, which was our second best, plain serge trousers and tunic; and, as was my chore, I cleaned the bell, which was done every morning. The weather in Scapa Flow was always a trifle on the wet side even when it was dry, but, having cleaned the bell, I went below to get dressed in No. 2 dress ready for Sunday divisions and prayers. This was my best uniform and the only one I was likely to get for the foreseeable future at that time. When I got back to the quarterdeck, the Officer of the watch, a RNVR Lieutenant, said,

"Bugler, you haven't cleaned the bell."

"Yes, I have, Sir," said I.

The atmosphere was so damp that the damned bell was dirty again thirty seconds after cleaning it, but he couldn't appreciate that.

"Clean it again," he said, and there I was in my best and only blue suit ready for divisions. Along came the Corporal of the gangway, an Irishman and always forthcoming with good advice when he wasn't involved:

"I'm . . . if I would clean it, Sticks."

So I went back to the Officer of the watch and told him that I wasn't going to clean the bell whilst in my best blue suit. He turned a shade of purple and eventually exploded and then charged me with mutiny.

When I appeared before Captain Wall (later Sir Patrick Wall, MP) the next morning it was obvious that he had his tongue in his cheek, but in my innocence I didn't know that and took it all very seriously. After reviewing the evidence against me, he asked if I wished to accept his punishment (seven days' No. 10 A,[1] loss of pay and shore leave and two hours' work in the evening) or be punished by Warrant; this meant cells for men, but for boys it was so many strokes of the cane administered by the Master at Arms in front of the whole Royal Marine detachment. Punishment by Warrant was always witnessed by the division concerned and was carried out over a box horse or some such apparatus; the boy would be wearing drill

---

[1] Punishments came under numerical sequence according to their severity, No. 1 being death by hanging.

trousers and the medical officer would be in attendance to observe that the skin was not broken and no blood came from the welt.

It was barbaric when one thinks about it, and directly descended from Nelson's era; nowadays the victim could sue in a court of law and probably be awarded a vast sum of money. I accepted Captain Wall's punishment but maybe I should have opted for the caning after all. This was still possible even in 1940; I don't know when it was eventually stopped.

The Sergeant-Major's Eggs

I mentioned earlier that someone noticed that I had not set foot on dry land for about nine months, but, as I said, there was nothing in Scapa Flow to attract a boy of my age, so why go? I had plenty of exercise running around this battleship all day, every day. I was struggling to reach five feet tall, every inch I put on I wore off on my legs. Nevertheless, as I have related, the Sergeant-Major was detailed to take me ashore and march me around the island of Hoy, which he did grudgingly and to my sorrow, but one good thing did come out of it — not for me, heaven forbid, but for the three Sergeants of the Sergeants' mess.

We came to an inhabited croft in the course of our completely conversationless march and there the Sergeant-Major succeeded in buying six new-laid eggs, as rare as jewels as we only had dried egg on board, and he managed to nursemaid them back to the ship. Cometh teatime, the three Sergeants decided to have them boiled for their tea and as usual it was "Sticks, take these six eggs up to the galley and get the cook to boil them for our tea." Notice that I was not included in this scrumptious feast. When I went in the galley the duty cook said, "I'm sorry, but the range is down", and as the ship dated back to 1913 there were no modern aids to cooking.

Being the master of innovation, the cook added, "Hang on, I know what we can do," and he fetched an empty 7lb jam tin, filled it with water and placed the eggs in it. The idea apparently was to put a steam hose into the water and blow steam in until the water boiled; this method was used to keep big vats of soup hot. Now who would have thought of that! Having inserted the steam tube, he cautiously opened the steam valve. There was an instant kerfuffle and, instead of blowing, it sucked and the water turned an ominous yolk colour.

"Oops," he said, "Never mind, there are two left."

"Two?" I said, "Two? There were six in there when I came in."

The thought of what the Sergeant-Major and the other Sergeants would do petrified me. I was so frightened that I didn't go back to the mess that evening, I hid. I knew where to hide if it was necessary. But by next morning I realized that, sooner or later, I would have to bite the bullet and take the consequences, so I meekly wandered back to the Sergeants' mess. The Sergeant-Major was not pleased, you could tell that by his face; after my long absence he had gone to the galley, heard what had happened and rescued *his* two eggs; the other Sergeants were in hysterics when I eventually went back.

It all ended happily — after all, who could have kept a straight face.

Where is the Anderson Shelter?

From time to time I made my escape from Scapa Flow.

In 1940 I was on my way home to Mitcham, on leave from HMS *Iron Duke*, and had boarded a Northern Line underground train to Tooting Broadway; suddenly we were all unceremoniously told to leave the train at Clapham South. A bomb had landed in the middle of Balham High Street and severed the water main, which had flooded Balham underground station. The station was sanctuary to hundreds of families from the nightly air raids and the platform would have been packed with sleeping bodies. To save further line flooding the fire/watertight doors at either end of the station were closed, so trapping all who were inside. I don't think they ever did find out how many people died there that night; some said 400, which I suspect was an exaggeration. But this meant that I had to walk from Clapham South to Mitcham, all of six miles or more, in pitch darkness and with a heavy air raid in progress (as it was every night from 7p.m.), so my walk home was accompanied by a certain amount of trepidation.

I was only fifteen years old. Bombs were falling all around and shrapnel from anti-aircraft guns added to the hazard. I had put on my steel helmet, which one carried at all times, together with a gas mask, a very small comfort in that hell of steel and explosives. The distance to walk was no problem but the bombing was; during an air raid it must be remembered that it is a very personal affair, the plane that is dropping its bombs is aiming directly at you, no one else. Even though it is dark, the bomb aimer can see you as plain as day, or so you think, and it is no comfort to remember the wiseacre who said that you never hear the one that hits you — something which no one has come back and confirmed, as far as I know.

Bombs were never dropped singly of course; the bomb aimer would press his little button and announce "Bombs gone", then he could hightail it back to where he had come from. It was completely indiscriminate so it became like Russian roulette — had he dropped four, five or six and were they coming towards us or going away? The civilians who suffered this night after night without breaking deserve more credit than they were given; many a serviceman would have broken, I'm sure.

When I eventually arrived home, I came in the back way across the open land that was there then and lo! the Anderson shelter was missing. It took me ten minutes to make someone hear me as I wasn't expected. The shelter, when you think of it now, was lamentable, even laughable if the situation wasn't so serious; it was cold, damp and uncomfortable, you were more likely to die of pneumonia or TB than from the effects of a bomb. The sirens sounded every night at 7p.m., just as supper was about to be served up, so everything had to be taken down to the end of the garden to the Anderson — saucepans, plates, cutlery — to be eaten whilst the enemy did his best to kill you.

Why put up with that? My father removed the floorboards in the back room, brought the Anderson indoors and sank it down to the foundations and then put the floorboards back, facing it directly on to the fire grate. It was as warm as toast and really comfortable, but I could never get rid of the idea that if we weren't blown to bits we would all burn anyway.

I was always pleased to get back to that battleship.

Funerals

Funerals — and here I was about to say at the best of times, but of course they are the worst of times — are always upsetting even though you may not be intimately involved. As a bugler I was often called upon to do a funeral but, as is generally the case, my first one was my worst.

It was in 1940 that a coastal minesweeper in the Pentland Firth struck one of the mines that it was sweeping for; it was only a small fishing drifter commandeered by the Royal Navy in those early days of the war when suitable craft were not available. I was told that it had sunk in about three minutes; the six members of the crew had no chance whatsoever, the Pentland Firth was not a stretch of water to sink in — the tide race there is phenomenal. The nearest place for the funeral was Scrabster, or was it Thurso or even Kirkwall?

As I was the nearest bugler in Scapa Flow on HMS *Iron Duke*, I found myself on another minesweeper bound for who knows where — this time an ex-Norwegian harpoon whaler, where I was welcomed by a huge Viking in thigh boots and horns growing out of his head. He was as surprised to see me as I was to see him and told me to go below. These boats were very sleek, very fast, very low in the water and very wet.

On arrival, we — that is the firing party and myself — were taken to the cemetery where "brass" and gold braid abounded, headed by the Officer in Charge of Coastal Forces (North), Rear-Admiral "Hooky" Walker. He was aptly nicknamed for the hook he had instead of his right hand. I was completely overawed and completely alone with my fear of all this ceremony, with no one to tell me what to do. I had never done anything like this in my life so far, I had never been to a funeral, I had never even seen a coffin before and here I was with six of them. I was terrified.

The mass funeral started and then it came to my solo pieces, "Last Post" and "Reveille". I started well but halfway through I could feel my lips turning to jelly until eventually I unashamedly burst into tears. Now, I thought, I'm for the chop, or hook as it was most likely to be in his case — but "Hooky" Walker, gentleman that he was, laid his hook on my shoulder and gently said "Never mind, laddie."

That was not my last funeral by a long way, all are upsetting, though you get blasé after a while. But it was an abiding memory that I shall never forget. I always wanted to go back, or even find someone who could tell me if that grave was still there.

POSTSCRIPT:
Some of the facts about the cause of death of the six men proved to be inexact, but it was the story that I

had been given to understand at the time. Research with the help of the Norwegian Ministry of Defence revealed the circumstances and history of the men concerned; the rest is true.

I did go back just a few years ago, found the graves at St Olaf's Cemetery in Kirkwall and across the deserted hills around Scapa Flow I whistled "Last Post". I'm too old to have the lungs for a bugle now, but I felt I had finally done my duty to those men.

HMS King George V

I served on the "Tin Duck" until March 1942, when I was returned to room B2, Eastney Barracks. I had been away the longest of all the boys and had by now become a veteran and an old soldier with many a tale to tell. I wasn't there long before I was drafted to HMS *King George V*, a 35,000-ton battleship of a new class, and where was she? Why, at Scapa Flow of course, but this time it was different, I had been blooded, I knew the sharp end from the blunt end and we were off on Arctic Convoys to Russia. Life became more varied. But I was always proud to say that I survived two years on the "Tin Duck" — so many didn't, many men suffered breakdowns, some volunteered for all sorts of dangerous things just to get off. But a young boy beat them all and came back sane.

My arrival at the *King George V* was something else. I was now sixteen years old and over five feet tall and was going to my second ship so I was regarded as an "old soldier" and knew what life was all about; but after the *Iron Duke* this was for real, the war had suddenly taken on a serious note.

The ship's boat collected us from the *St Ninian*, which had brought us over from Scrabster. The enormous grey battleship looked awesome as we pulled alongside it and my heart was in my boots; and yet somehow the transition was a lot easier. The strict naval discipline that I had been subject to on the "Tin Duck" was very much relaxed here. A large proportion of the men were hostilities-only men, working a wartime seagoing routine — they would never have suffered that kind of discipline happily.

There was a Royal Marine band on board as well, as there was on most capital ships (by which I mean cruisers, aircraft carriers and battleships), so we Boy Buglers were put in the band mess and had the company of thirty other messmates. Life was certainly better, even the food was better, and to work on a ship with a definite routine was better — it was indeed a lot more enjoyable.

The ship was taking part in shadowing the Arctic Convoys at the time; there were four of the King George class, split into two groups which took it in turns to cover a convoy up to Russia and back. HMS *Howe* was our sister ship together with the aircraft carrier *Victorious*; the other group was the *Duke of York* and the *Anson* and our job was to get between the convoy and the Norwegian coast in case the German battleship *Tirpitz* ever put to sea. She never did so our main danger was from mines, aircraft and U-boats. Once above the Arctic Circle our biggest enemy was the cold and the weather as this was winter and the war at sea was never cancelled because the conditions were bad. On leaving the comparative safety of Scapa Flow we were subject to all these hazards and life became a round of on-watch on the bridge or sleeping, four hours on and four hours off.

We were generally spotted by a German reconnaissance plane soon after leaving harbour, a Fokke-Wulf would shadow us way out of range; we knew he was there and he knew where we were and was obviously relaying our position back to the Fatherland. The cold was just about bearable; we would pile on any clothing that we could find and must have looked like a bunch of pirates — gone were the smartness and discipline; once we crossed the Arctic Circle men were discouraged from shaving until we got back again as this made the facial skin more tender and the time normally taken having a shower could be spent in sleep.

The upper deck very soon became encrusted with ice from the sea spray, which had to be constantly cleared, not only to keep the guns in a workable condition but also because too much ice could make the ship unstable, so there was always work to be done. The lookouts on the bridge, of which there were three on either side, could only manage twenty-minute spells and then had to be relieved to find shelter and warm up a bit before the next one. If we were lucky, the convoy would get past Norway and into Russian waters and we would leave them and patrol around Jan Mayan and Bear Island in the pack ice to wait for a returning convoy to get back home.

We did this for about six months when the rumours began to spread that we were going to the Mediterranean and sure enough, just after Christmas 1942, which we spent at sea, we sailed for Rosyth for a quick refit and some leave; and we set off for sunnier climes. Together with the *Howe* again, we formed Force Z based at Algiers and Oran — much better than the Arctic.

POSTSCRIPT:

In nearly all the campaigns of World War Two, the men who served were awarded a campaign medal; an exception to this was the Arctic Convoys — even though no operation was more worthy of commemoration. It was dangerous, it was cold and it was bitter; the conditions were the worst of all the campaigns at sea. If your ship was sunk, and you entered the water, it was estimated that it was only three minutes before your heart stopped in shock; this was ever present in your mind.

To give some sort of recognition to the men who served in those circumstances, the Arctic Association was formed and a lapel badge, the Arctic Star, awarded, and as a mark of distinction a white beret could be worn. It isn't truly white, actually; it has a yellow shading to denote the fact that blood turns yellow when frozen on ice. White berets are now hard to find; I was told that the Association had six left and that the only people who applied nowadays were relatives who wanted them for the funeral of an old Arctic Campaigner.

For me it is something that I am proud to possess and wear on ceremonial occasions — and to be alive to do so, of course.

Messdeck Life

I suppose it was late in my life — I must have been at least sixteen — before I had the chance to experience life on a messdeck. As I have mentioned, whilst aboard HMS *Iron Duke* I was made to live in the Sergeants' mess; I wasn't allowed to mix with the grown-ups, the Marines on their messdeck.

When I went to HMS *King George V* life became very different to what I had been used to. I was now an "old hand", streetwise in every way and quite capable of looking after myself, knowing where the dangers lay; also the ship had a Royal Marines band aboard. It was not a large band, about twenty-five musicians, but they did have their own secluded messdeck — that is if anywhere on a battleship called be labelled secluded. We were separate from the main messdecks, however; this was where we lived, ate, slept and spent most of our spare time. Food was fetched from the galley, served up and eaten on two long mess tables. We all slept in hammocks then, of course, and I have to say that they were very comfortable and warm; you found your own billet in which to sling your hammock and this became yours for as long as you were on the ship.

There was a certain tradition about slinging your hammock, a skill not easily learnt, especially in the mornings when "Reveille" was sounded together with the order to "Heave Ho, Lash Up and Stow". The two blankets (we were not issued with sheets) together with all the head and foot lashings were folded inside the hammock, which was then roped up using the traditional seven hitches, no more, no less, then placed in the hammock "netting". I believe that description came from the days of the old wooden ships when before action all the hammocks were stowed in netting along the ship's side as protection from musket shot and splinters.

Personal lockers were also on the messdeck. In them you kept all the day-to-day possessions that were required and, as I remember, they were seldom locked. All your clothing had to be marked with your name and regimental number, of course — if it wasn't then you only had yourself to blame if it disappeared; but in the main your personal possessions were quite safe, things could be left on the mess table (though this was not encouraged) and would not be touched or removed.

There was a code of honour on the messdeck, where men had to live together for maybe two years or more; a thief would not be tolerated and if ever the code was broken — and I cannot recall that ever happening — the thief would be hounded out, publicly named and his life would be a misery henceforth. Again, I suppose that is what camaraderie was all about. There had to be trust among one another for it to work.

The Cross Country Race

It was 4 November 1942 and HMS *King George V* was between Arctic Convoys — I know it was then as it says so on the certificate that I earned that day. Some bright spark had the idea that we should have an inter-part of the ship cross country race, as maybe we needed the exercise and fresh air. Personally, I'd had enough of that on our journeys northwards. As we were in Scapa Flow, the race was to be about eight miles around Flotta, a barren little island in those days but it was now home to the fleet canteen, which was the only place we were allowed ashore and had a facility to show films.

Naturally, the Royal Marines were expected to enter a team and I have a suspicion that the Sergeant-Major didn't get the overwhelming response he had anticipated, so, thinking of ways to make up the numbers, he reckoned, aha! those two lazy Boy Buglers could do with some fresh air. The indignity of it, if anyone got exercise it was Curly Regan and me but, brushing aside all our protestations, he said, "Get your gym shoes, shorts and vest and get there!"

The race would start from the fleet canteen, which had the only road on the island, then strike off into the countryside for a distance of eight miles. Off we went. After about half a mile Curly and I spotted a dilapidated croft, of which there were many on the island. We had long since agreed that we were not running eight miles if we could help it, so we slid off and hid in the croft with our fags and matches. It was a circular route which came back to the road for the finish, and after about an hour the leaders were nearing home, so we let them pass until it was down to the "tail end Charlies", then we joined in and rushed to the finishing line to be out of breath and red in the face. We weren't last (next to last maybe), but definitely not last, and we complained bitterly that it hadn't been fair as we were two boys up against grown men. We were told to stop moaning and get back to the ship.

When we arrived back on board the prizes were being given out and apparently the Royal Marines team had come in first. As Curly and I were part of the Royal Marines team we proudly received our certificates from Captain Mack, a giant of a man and looking every inch a Royal Navy Sea Captain, but Curly and I had great difficulty in hiding our hysterics. Captain Mack left us shortly afterwards to take up a job liaising with the American forces in North Africa, where he was killed in an air crash.

A Convoy to Russia

It was New Year's Eve 1942 when we left Scapa Flow to cover Convoy JW 53. They were given those prefixes, JW for going up, RA for coming home. HMS *King George V* together with *Howe*, *Sheffield* and *Berwick* and the aircraft carrier *Victorious* slipped out of the Flow and headed north. Our job was to get between the convoy and the Norwegian coast as it was thought that the *Tirpitz* was preparing to put to sea. We would cover the convoy up as far as Kola inlet and then patrol around Jan Mayan island on the edge of the pack ice to await the RA convoy going home.

The moment we left Scapa Flow we knew we were in for a good hiding; the weather was atrocious, but go we must. The further north we went the worse the weather got until we were in a full-force hurricane with winds off the Beaufort scale. I have never seen waves of the like since; looking from the bridge of *King George V* they were level with our eyes, and when you imagine that every wave of forty to fifty feet has a trough of a similar depth there were many times when, seeing a wave like that coming towards the bows, we could be forgiven for thinking that she would never make this one.

But they were sturdy ships, and make it they did, even though the damage was considerable. We lost most of our upper-deck boats and light anti-aircraft guns on the bows and the ventilation covers were torn off, which meant flooding of the mess decks to a foot deep and everyone having to live with their trousers rolled up. HMS *Sheffield* had the top of "A" turret ripped off like a tin of sardines; any thoughts of protecting the convoy went by the board, for no self-respecting enemy would put to sea in that weather. In all, I think it was known as the worst weather ever encountered by a Russian convoy. Our task force gave up and headed for the safety of Iceland were we had three major bases, Hval Fjord, Seydis Fjord and Akureyri Fjord, which is just above the Arctic Circle.

The fjord leading to Akureyri was the most beautiful sight I have ever seen. I believe it is thirty-two miles long between enormous snow-covered mountains which dwarfed the fjord until our enormous ships looked like so many twigs floating down a stream. The houses in the town itself all had different coloured roofs, making a glorious patchwork. I have always wanted to go back as we weren't really welcome then; after all we were an occupying force in a way, deciding to set up bases before the Germans did.

My photo, with one of the seaman buglers, was taken when we were anchored in Akureyri. Smoking again — we all did that.

Two memories of Russian convoys stay in my mind. One is the constant ice and cold. Nowhere could you get warm. The other is that, if when eating a meal you were up against the ship's side, you could feel the sea thumping against it and hear it swishing past, and you had the ever present thought that three inches of steel was all there was between you and a torpedo or a mine at any time, not only then but at all times when at sea. It didn't do to let the mind dwell on that too much.

Hands to Bathe

On each capital ship there were always two Royal Marine buglers, most aged between fourteen and eighteen. There were some who remained buglers and were therefore over eighteen. We were supplemented by two Royal Navy buglers, also boys, but boys in the Navy didn't go to sea much before the age of sixteen. A photograph shows one of us (Curly Regan) together with the two Royal Navy buglers we had aboard HMS *King George V*; the four of us could never be seen together at any one time as one was always away on watch. We could work a four-watch system whereby for twenty-four hours you did four hours on and four hours off, then there was a twenty-four-hour break before another twenty-four hours, four on, four off, then a thirty-two-hour break before starting all over again, day in day out.

I regret that I cannot after all these years remember the names of the two Royal Navy buglers but the photo brings back a sad memory concerning the boy on the right. We were in Gibraltar, moored up to the "Mole", and that day I was the bugler of the watch from 16.00 hours to 20.00 hours, known as the dog watches. After a hot, sweaty day, at 17.00 hours was piped "Hands to Bathe", which meant that you could go over the ship's side for a swim if you so wished. As a rule, with a shout of "Geronimo" (what an Apache war chief had to do with it, I don't know) most would stop what they were doing and either jump or dive over the ship's side.

On the quarterdeck where I was on watch we received a telephone message saying "a bloke has dived over the side from the fo'c'sle [the bows] and ain't not came up yet" (I think the caller was a Scouser). "Don't be ridiculous, that's not funny," said the young naval Lieutenant. After ten minutes we had another message to say "that bloke ain't came up yet, you know", by which time the Lieutenant realized that he had dropped a goolie and took it very seriously. But who was the man who had dived over the side? How could you tell from 1,500 men? The only way was to sound "Clear Lower Deck, Hands to Divisions", whereby the whole ship's company could be mustered and accounted for. When this had been completed, indeed one man was missing and it was the Navy bugler who was due to relieve me on watch at 20.00 hours, the boy on the right of the photo.

Despite divers searching, his body was never found. The bows of HMS *King George V* must have been at least thirty-five feet high and it was thought that he broke his back on the way down and his body was taken by the tide out into the bay. The bugler was impossible to replace under the circumstances as we were out and about all over the Mediterranean, so we had to work a three-watch system, which was a bit difficult.

A lighter sequel to this happened in later years. I was on HMS *Glasgow* in the Indian Ocean in 1946 — no submarine problem then of course. We had stopped mid-ocean and piped "Hands to Bathe". I was nonchalantly swimming along when the man next to me said, "Do you realize that the seabed is three miles down?" Blind panic took hold and I have never got out of water so quickly since.

The Beginning of the End

It was on 5 April 1943 that I had my eighteenth birthday. I was now no longer a boy. I was a man, I'd known that for a long time as I had started to shave. My conduct and character assessments on my Service Sheets were blotted out with Indian ink so I started my twelve-year engagement with a clean sheet; I wonder if that is where the old saying "starting with a clean sheet" comes from. My pay now went from 1s (5p) to 3s (15p) a day, a fortune to me, and I suppose I must have been given all those 1s 9d that had been saved for a "rainy day", which I calculate would have come to £22 6s 3d — not that I can honestly remember having received such a large sum of money, which to someone who had never ever seen a white £5 note in his life was a huge amount.

It was also when I had to decide whether to remain a bugler or "transfer to the ranks" and become a fully fledged Marine. I wasted no time in forwarding my request to transfer to the ranks but was informed that I couldn't be returned to Eastney Barracks as we were in the Mediterranean and I would have to wait until we were sent home — I didn't know then that we had the

Sicily and Italian Campaigns yet to come, so that wouldn't be until October 1943. Even then, at Christmas we went back to the Mediterranean to fetch Winston Churchill after he caught pneumonia whilst at Marrakesh, and then we did one more convoy north before going into dry dock at Liverpool, so it was March 1944 before I finally left HMS *King George V*. I was sad in a way as I had enjoyed every moment on that ship; it was "a happy ship", not all of them were, but by this time I was nearly nineteen.

When I arrived back in Eastney Barracks I joined up with two other buglers whom I knew who had also transferred; one, Peter Baxter, was a survivor at fifteen years of age from HMS *Barham*. I'm sure many people have seen the film footage of the *Barham*, having been torpedoed, keeling over on to her side and then blowing up in one massive explosion as her magazines went up. Peter still had wounds to show, but never knew how he survived; one moment he was eating his tea, the next he was in the water.

As we were three old hands by now, we had to wait for the next squad in training which we could join when they were six months on — there was no point in drilling us in the basics because we had been doing them for the past five years. My training finished in February 1944, and I was very soon drafted to HMS *Glasgow*, a 10,000-ton cruiser, as a trained Marine. She was in the Swan Hunter shipyard in Hebburn on Tyne for repairs after damage at the D-day landings and was being refitted for the Far East, which was where we knew we were going.

At this point let me say that I am not sorry or have any feelings of guilt for what we did at Hiroshima and Nagasaki; we were on our way for landings in Japan eventually, when tens of thousands of men would be killed on both sides. For the first three months after we arrived in the Far East we were ferrying ex-POWs from Singapore to Colombo in Ceylon (as it was then) for shipment home, and I saw what those poor devils had endured. If we had not dropped the bombs would I have survived, would my son and daughter have been born, would my grandchildren have existed, would I have been here to write this? Probably not. No, I am not sorry and feel no guilt.

The Spitkid Sentry

Once World War Two had ended, the Royal Navy wasted no time in trying to get back to its pre-war glory — not that it was ever going to work again, discipline had been relaxed by circumstances and also a new generation had come along who had no experience of the blind sub-servience of the pre-war years — but try it did.

HMS *Glasgow* was, as I have said, being refitted for service in the Pacific, which we all knew meant the invasion of Japan. The end of the war in Europe was celebrated whilst we were in dock, but our war was not yet over, or so we thought. We eventually sailed from England for a two-year commission, possibly longer, on 15 August 1945, a week after the A-bomb was dropped on Hiroshima and the day after Japan had surrendered, but our destination and job had been hurriedly changed due to the circumstances. We were now going to Ceylon as flagship of the East Indies Fleet, to be based at Trincomalee. On the way our Executive Officer, Commander John Bruce Goodenough Temple (what a lovely name), did his best to lick us all back into shape and something like a peacetime Navy. Decks were scrubbed daily, the quarterdeck was holystoned, the ship lost its camouflage appearance and was painted in the East Indies colour of white with yellow funnels. I believe the Officers paid to have the after gun turret painted with white enamel. We looked very smart and something like a pre-war ship.

During the course of the day's work we were allowed a break for tea and a smoke if wanted, known as a "Stand Easy", and work was resumed at "Out Pipes" (I suppose that expression came from the days before cigarettes were fashionable and most men either smoked a pipe or chewed tobacco, a disgusting habit). We were not allowed to smoke below decks at "Stand Easy" and as the upper decks were regularly scrubbed, they had to be kept immaculate — no stubbing out of fag ends or flicking dud matches away now, this is where the "spitkid sentry" came in.

A spitkid is an aluminium bowl shaped like an urn and into it went all cigarette ends, matches and spittle from the tobacco chewers — it was an offence to miss. So someone who had committed a misdemeanour was given a Naval Police armband and a walking stick, and when "Stand Easy, Place Spitkids" was sounded on the bugle, it was his job to forego his stand easy, don the armband and walking stick and patrol the upper deck until he could catch someone missing the spitkid, when he was authorized to hand over the armband and walking stick to a successor. The practice never lasted, though, as there was a much bigger ashtray over the ship's side — the whole of the Indian Ocean, in fact.

Postscript

On 5 March 1955 my twelve-year engagement was at an end. I had a month's leave to take me up to my thirtieth birthday. Prior to my leaving I had the usual interview, which was meant to encourage one to sign on further for a pension in another nine years. I had no intention of doing so as I had already served sixteen years. In any case I was told that "I would not be invited to sign on for a pension" as I had lost all hearing in my right ear. Remember the guns? This deafness had been caused by wartime activity and eventually I received a small war pension for it almost forty years later.

When it had been realized in 1950 that I was deaf on one side, I was told to prepare to be medically discharged within six weeks; but then the powers that be decided that I was "an asset even with one ear", which — due to the circumstances at the time — I suppose I was. But now, having used my "assets" for the past five years, I was not being "invited" to sign on for a pension.

The morning I walked out of Eastney Barracks was a black day in a way; this was the only life I had ever

98

known. For years, in between ships, the barracks had been my home and the men in it were my family, but by now I had a family of my own. Standing outside the gates, I was completely bemused and afraid, with no idea how I was going to support my wife Vera, a four year old son Malcolm, and eighteen month old daughter Lynne. No preparation or counselling whatsoever and no job lined up, they never even came to say goodbye.

In my hand I had a small cardboard attaché case, eighteen inches by ten I suppose, and in it were all my worldly possessions. Looking back at the barracks I thought, what have I got to show for sixteen years, all of World War Two and the Far East? I had one month's wages, one month's ration money, a single ticket to Exeter Central station and a letter in my pocket which said that if I didn't return my uniform within fourteen days, I would be charged for it.

That was my reward for sixteen years. I am so pleased to know that everything is much better now. It surely needed to be.

Remembrance Day, November 2006

ISIS publish a wide range of books in large print, from fiction to biography. Any suggestions for books you would like to see in large print or audio are always welcome. Please send to the Editorial Department at:

ISIS Publishing Limited
7 Centremead
Osney Mead
Oxford OX2 0ES

A full list of titles is available free of charge from:

Ulverscroft Large Print Books Limited

(UK)
The Green
Bradgate Road, Anstey
Leicester LE7 7FU
Tel: (0116) 236 4325

(Australia)
P.O. Box 314
St Leonards
NSW 1590
Tel: (02) 9436 2622

(USA)
P.O. Box 1230
West Seneca
N.Y. 14224-1230
Tel: (716) 674 4270

(Canada)
P.O. Box 80038
Burlington
Ontario L7L 6B1
Tel: (905) 637 8734

(New Zealand)
P.O. Box 456
Feilding
Tel: (06) 323 6828

Details of **ISIS** complete and unabridged audio books are also available from these offices. Alternatively, contact your local library for details of their collection of **ISIS** large print and unabridged audio books.